Top 10 Ways To Be A Great Leader

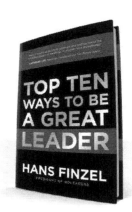

A Listening Guide & Workbook

This workbook is designed as a companion to the book, Top Ten Ways To Be A Great Leader (David C Cook 2017) — Available in print, audiobook and Kindle

© 2018 Top Ten Enterprises
9457 S University #712
Highlands Ranch, CO 80126-4976

About Hans Finzel

Dr. Hans Finzel is a successful author, speaker and trusted authority in the field of leadership. For 20 years he served as President of international non-profit WorldVenture, working in over 65 countries. Hans speaks, writes and teaches on practical leadership principles from the real world—not just the classroom. He is a graduate of Columbia International University, Dallas Seminary and Fuller School of Intercultural Studies.

He has written eleven books, including his bestseller, "The Top Ten Mistakes Leaders Make" (David C Cook). Hans has trained leaders on five continents and his books have been translated into over twenty foreign languages. Today he serves as President of HDLeaders and teaches and speaks globally on all things leadership.   Hans and his wife Donna have four grown children and make their home in Colorado.

Contact Hans at hansfinzel.com
Twitter: hansfinzel
Facebook: facebook.com/hansfinzel
YouTube: youtube.com/hansfinzel

To Benefit from
"Top Ten Ways To Be A Great Leader" Listening Guide

- Introduce yourself to Hans Finzel
- Mute your cell phone please
- Participate with other attendees in discussions and answering questions
- Take notes and fill in the blanks in this workbook
- Look for major "Aha moments" and highlight those in your notes
- Be sure and stop by the book table and grab some other great leadership resources
- Take time to discuss your takeaways with your team over a meal in the next week

What Others Say About
Top Ten Ways To Be A Great Leader

"Hans Finzel has the broadest grasp of leadership of any person I have encountered. He relates leadership to the real world in such practical terms. I've had so much fun reading this, his newest book on leadership, because Hans is a truly brilliant communicator. Over the years, Hans's influence has made me the leader that I am, and I continue to follow his advice and use his insights. He looks at all aspects of leadership and is always adding the best to his toolbox. He then passes those tools on in a fun-to-follow way."

Kathrine Lee
Founder of Pure Hope Foundation, life coach, business strategist,
and creator of The Ultimate Source

"Many equate leadership with knowledge or talent, but in today's workplace people don't necessarily follow knowledge or talent. Both are easy to find, and having them may actually be a deterrent to effective leadership. Top Ten Ways to Be a Great Leader shows us the characteristics that real leaders possess. And fortunately, they can be learned by anyone with a heart for true leadership."

Dan Miller, career coach, bestselling author,
and President of 48 Days LLC

"Whenever my friend Hans Finzel writes or speaks about leadership, he has my full attention. His insights are compelling because they are grounded in truth, tested by experience, and on full display in and through his life and ministry."

Dr. Crawford W. Loritts, Jr., author, speaker, radio host,
and senior pastor of Fellowship Bible Church, Roswell, GA

"When Hans Finzel wrote his bestselling book, The Top Ten Mistakes That Leaders Make, I thought it was one of the greatest leadership books of all time. I have been greatly impacted by it over the years! His newest book, Top Ten Ways to Be a Great Leader, is destined to be a best seller because it is down-to-earth practical and is based on Hans's many years of leadership experience. I highly recommend it to anyone interested in becoming a great leader or anyone wanting to develop leaders who can make a difference in a world that is desperate for character-based leadership."

Stan Toler, bestselling author and speaker

Top Ten Ways To Be A Great Leader
A Listening Guide and Workbook

Table of Contents

Top Ten Ways To Be A Great Leader

An Introduction to Leaders and Leadership

Definition: "Leadership is *influence*."
- Anyone who influences someone else to do something has led that person.
- *A leader takes people where they would never go on their own."*

Leadership Axioms: Six observations about leadership in general

1. If you do what comes natural _____

2. People are confused _____. We _____ as we were _____.

3. Just because you are in a position of leadership, _____.

4. It takes more than _____to be a great Christian leader.

5. There seem to be more bad _____and _____ than _____ ones.

6. The world needs more great _____.

> After 30 years in the trenches of leadership, I decided to ask the question, "What are the most important skills every new leader should master?" I came up with an acrostic for the word LEADERSHIP. Each chapter of this book, 10 chapters in all, outlines an essential skill every leader must master. The "*Top 10 Mistakes Leaders Make*" is about pitfalls to avoid. This book is about essential skills every leader needs to be successful. – Hans Finzel

Chapter One
"L" Is for Listen and Learn.

The "L" in leadership stands for two massively important words—*listen and learn.* It has been my observation that one greatly affects the other. People who don't do well with the one generally don't practice the other. If you are not willing to be a lifelong learner, why should you listen to great ideas from other people? Conversely, can you learn and grow without listening?

The higher you go in leadership, the more you're isolated and insulated from those people on the front lines

Why it's tough for busy leaders to listen well

1. Too little _____

2. Too many _____

3. Too much _____

4. Too big of a _____

5. Too much _____

The Kernel of Wisdom: The two most important words in a leader's vocabulary are *listen and learn.*

How do you feel if I am not listened to?

I feel...

How do I feel when I am listened to?

1. Unimportant	1. _____
2. Marginalized	2. _____
3. Waste of time trying	3. _____
4. I am invisible	4. _____
5. My opinions are not respected	5. _____
6. I am not respected	6. _____
7. I have nothing to contribute	7. _____
8. Nothing is going to change	8. _____

Source: *Three Signs of a Miserable Job*, Patrick Lencioni (Jossy-Bass)

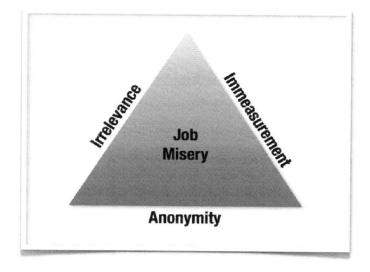

Not Just Listen....
Keep Learning!

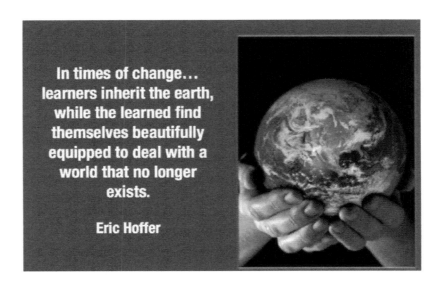

In times of change... learners inherit the earth, while the learned find themselves beautifully equipped to deal with a world that no longer exists.

Eric Hoffer

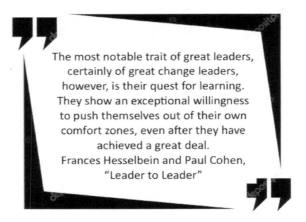

The most notable trait of great leaders, certainly of great change leaders, however, is their quest for learning. They show an exceptional willingness to push themselves out of their own comfort zones, even after they have achieved a great deal.
Frances Hesselbein and Paul Cohen, "Leader to Leader"

Action Points and Discussion Questions

1. Sharpen your listening skills with feedback.

2. Try feeding back to people what they said to you.

3. There is no substitute for "face time" with your team.

4. Consume a regular diet of resources that help you grow.

Chapter Two
"E" Is for Emotional Intelligence

The "E" in leadership stands for emotional intelligence. It's known as EQ as opposed to IQ, which is our intelligence quotient. Success in leadership has so much more to do with EQ than IQ. "The ability to *know one's self as well as what others are perceiving about us* is paramount to understanding if and when to move forward with a proposed plan or how to go about engaging with the varying personalities that compose a team."

Your IQ is what people usually see first, above the water line. But it is your EQ that matters the most as a leader... remember that the Titanic was sunk by many cuts from the iceberg below the waterline!

Emotional Intelligence Definition

The capacity to be aware of, control, and express _____ and to handle _____ judiciously and empathetically.

The ability to know one's self as well as what others are _____ about us.

The Kernel of Wisdom: It is EQ that has the *biggest impact on long-term effectiveness* in a job—and in success as a leader.

Five building Blocks of Your Emotional Intelligence

1. Self _____

2. Self _____

3. _____

4. _____ making

5. _____ management

How Can I Improve My EQ?

1. Take an _____ on line

2. Read a good book on EQ.

3. Try some _____.

4. Ask the "_____?" question of your staff

5. Try a _____ degree evaluation (But be careful)

> Emotional intelligence is the "something" in each of us that is a bit intangible. It affects how we manage behavior, navigate social complexities, and make personal decisions that achieve positive results. Emotional intelligence is made up of four core skills that pair up under two primary competencies: *personal competence* and *social competence*.
>
> Source: http://www.talentsmart.com/

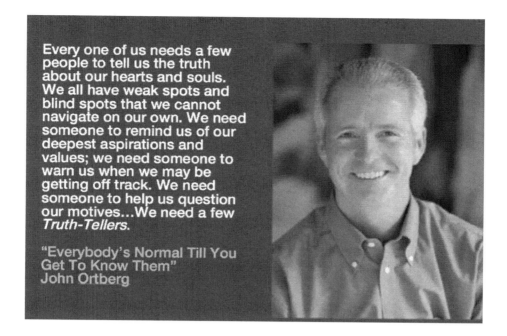

Every one of us needs a few people to tell us the truth about our hearts and souls. We all have weak spots and blind spots that we cannot navigate on our own. We need someone to remind us of our deepest aspirations and values; we need someone to warn us when we may be getting off track. We need someone to help us question our motives...We need a few *Truth-Tellers*.

"Everybody's Normal Till You Get To Know Them"
John Ortberg

Action Points and Discussion Questions

1. Take the free EQ quiz at myframeworks.org or bit.ly/eqtesting

2. Read a good book on Emotional Intelligence. (Page 38)

3. Perform some simple evaluations of your own leadership and your team.

4. Listen to a couple of my podcasts where I interview experts on Emotional Intelligence.

Chapter Three
"A" Is for Accessibility

The "A" in leadership stands for *accessibility*. Did you know that accessibility is absolutely essential for today's leaders? Gone are the corner offices and executive floors. People, especially the younger generations, demand to have access to their team leaders. Along with accessibility, there is a partner word that is just as crucial today: *vulnerability*. One of the biggest mistakes you can make as a new leader starting out is isolation and insulation from your team. If you are used to working alone, this can be a *huge* adjustment for you when all of a sudden, other people are looking to you for leadership and they are invading your space. Worst yet, they might be asking you personal and probing questions that make you feel uncomfortable.

Power distance is a term that describes how people belonging to a specific culture view power relationships.

CONCEPTS OF POWER DISTANCE

©study.c

Individuals in cultures demonstrating a _____ are very deferential to figures of authority and generally accept an unequal distribution of power, while individuals in cultures demonstrating a _____ readily question authority and expect to participate in decisions that affect them. From Geert Hofstede's **Cultural Dimensions Theory**

The Kernel of Wisdom: Today's effective leaders have to be *accessible and vulnerable* to their flock weather they are comfortable with it or not.

What do Millennials want in their leaders? (Page 67)

They want a leader who is _____ versus _____

They appreciate leaders who are _____

Life on Life Discipleship

Paul, another one of my favorite leaders in all the New Testament, had a "life on life" style of leadership. He had no corner office, he had no ivory tower, he had no pulpit or lectern that he hid behind. His work, his ministry as a leader, was life on life.

> 1 Thessalonians 2:7-8 says, "But we proved to be gentle among you, as a nursing mother tenderly cares for her own children. Having so fond an affection for you we were well pleased to impart to you not only the gospel of God (meaning the knowledge, the information), **but also our own lives** because you had become very dear to us."

The Power of Vulnerability

Vulnerability comes from the Latin word for "wound," *vulnus*. Vulnerability is the state of being open to injury, or appearing as if you are. It might be emotional, like admitting that you're in love with someone who might only like you as a friend, or it can be literal, like the vulnerability of a soccer goal that's unprotected by any defensive players.

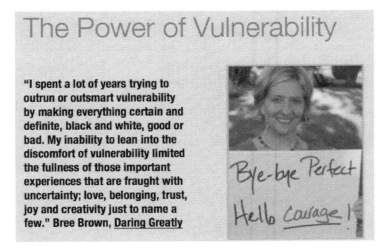

The Power of Vulnerability

"I spent a lot of years trying to outrun or outsmart vulnerability by making everything certain and definite, black and white, good or bad. My inability to lean into the discomfort of vulnerability limited the fullness of those important experiences that are fraught with uncertainty; love, belonging, trust, joy and creativity just to name a few." Bree Brown, Daring Greatly

Bye-bye Perfect
Hello Courage !

Exercise on Vulnerability

How do you define vulnerability?

_____

Does it come easy for you? _____

Why or why not? _____

Share this with your neighbor

Action Points and Discussion Questions

Accessibility....

1. Be sure you have times when you're accessible to your people.

2. When you need to be alone, structure it and let people know you'll get back to them.

Vulnerability....

3. Don't pretend to be perfect or to have your entire act together.

4. Watch the YouTube TED talk by Brené Brown on "The Power of Vulnerability."

Chapter Four
"D" Is for Determination

Courageous leadership is a great quality of leaders that endure. It is another way to talk about determination—because determination requires courage.

Sometimes bad things happen to good people. It is impossible to "failure proof" our lives, and that's certainly true of our journey as leaders. We all face tough times. *Success is not the absence of failure, it is persistence through failure.*

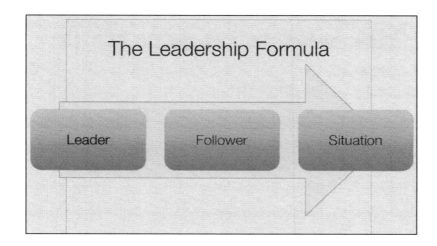

In addition to these three factors, what else overlays success and/or failure in ministry for Christian leaders?

- The _____

- The _____

 The Kernel of Wisdom: "A dream doesn't become reality through magic; *it takes sweat, determination and hard work.*" General Colin Powell

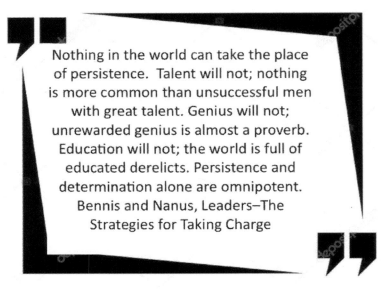

Nothing in the world can take the place of persistence. Talent will not; nothing is more common than unsuccessful men with great talent. Genius will not; unrewarded genius is almost a proverb. Education will not; the world is full of educated derelicts. Persistence and determination alone are omnipotent. Bennis and Nanus, Leaders—The Strategies for Taking Charge

What factors in your life right now are providing strong resistance to you achieving all that you desire?

1. _____

2. _____

3. _____

Action Points and Discussion Questions

1. Try this first: trust God.
2. Trust yourself.
3. Remember that "this too shall pass."
4. Be connected in a community with people that will help you keep going.
5. Read the book or listen to the audiobook *The Resistance* by Stephen Pressfield
6. Commit to Massive Action.

Chapter Five
"E" Is for Effective Communication

Learn to over-communicate by a factor of ten. Speak, rinse, and repeat. Everyone you work with struggles with tech clutter. The emails, texts, blogs, IMs, Facebook and Twitter posts, and you name it all create background noise that makes it tough for your message to get through. You will never over-communicate. I don't think that is possible.

Try the 3 by 5 card exercise: (Pass out 3x5 Cards)

1. Can you write down the vision of your ministry in a few sentences?
   Or try this instead:
2. Dear Leaders, I would like to know more about...

 The Kernel of Wisdom: *Never assume that anyone knows anything.* Over communicate to your people by a factor of ten.

If there is mist in the pulpit there is fog in the pew

ALIGNMENT
Alignment and clarity cannot be achieved in one fell swoop with a series of generic buzzwords and aspirational phrases crammed together.
- Patrick Lencioni "The Advantage"

Why Don't Most Leaders Communicate Enough?

Most leaders don't communicate enough. It is amazing how many leaders think that the troops know what is going on when in reality, they really are totally in the dark. Sometimes the leader thinks that the communication happens magically through osmosis. Other times they think that they communicated to all when they really communicated with just a few. (Only the inner circle is informed)

1. Too little _____

2. Too many _____

3. _____

4. _____

5. Too much _____

6. _____

7. Communication _____

What Must I Communicate to My Team?

1. Communicate the _____.

2. Communicate concrete _____ and _____.

3. Be sure to communicate _____and _____when needed.

4. Troll for _____ from your team—never make all communication

    one-way.

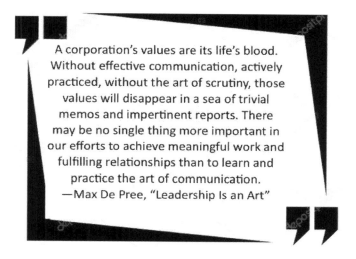

A corporation's values are its life's blood. Without effective communication, actively practiced, without the art of scrutiny, those values will disappear in a sea of trivial memos and impertinent reports. There may be no single thing more important in our efforts to achieve meaningful work and fulfilling relationships than to learn and practice the art of communication.
—Max De Pree, "Leadership Is an Art"

Review the 3x5 Card exercise results

Action Points and Discussion Questions

1. Share the vision, rinse, and repeat.

2. Remember that face time makes or breaks your communication with your team.

3. Communicate in writing, not just orally.

4. Try the 3x5 card exercise.

5. Listen to my podcast titled "Care enough to confront."

Chapter 6
"R" Is for Resilience

The "R" in LEADERSHIP stands for resilience. Resilience means that you are pliable, flexible, and able to bend—like a healthy cherry tree. Every new leader must develop the practice of becoming resilient.

Resilience is a softening effect. It's being soft in spirit, not rigid. It's like a young sapling that is healthy, flexible, and alive no matter how strong the wind blows. Being a leader who displays resilience is not being spineless—it is being responsive to the changing world in which we have to lead our team.

Leading people in the journey of change is a lot like this Slinky. Can you live with ambiguity as you lead your team, or do you tilt toward being a control freak? Today's effective leaders have to learn to be resilient as massive agents of change.

What is Resilience?

Able to withstand or recover quickly from _____.
Able to _____ into shape after bending, stretching, or being compressed.
Resilience is about our capacity _____ from difficulties, disappointments, heartbreak, and hard times. It's the ability to _____.

The Kernel of Wisdom: *Resilience—the ability to flex and bounce back--is absolutely critical in most endeavors; in leadership and in life.*

The Difference Between Resilience and Persistence

Sometimes we have persistence but we lack resilience, and we really need to have both; it's like two sides of a coin.

Resilience is absolutely critical in most endeavors; in leadership, in our lives. Persistence keeps us in the race, but resilience returns us to the right path when we get knocked off course, even when we get knocked to the ground."

Source: *Bouncing Back*, Blog by David Beavers. August 28, 2013

Five Characteristics of Resilient People

Resilient people have the ability to deal with difficult times and still show progress in their lives. Resilient people have five characteristics in common:

1) They use their _____,

2) They _____ when it's needed,

3) They _____ of coping,

4) They have _____ and

5) They stay _____ to others.

Brene Brown
The Gifts of Imperfection,
Chapter Six, Hazelden, 2010)

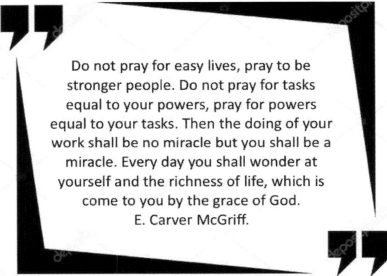

Do not pray for easy lives, pray to be stronger people. Do not pray for tasks equal to your powers, pray for powers equal to your tasks. Then the doing of your work shall be no miracle but you shall be a miracle. Every day you shall wonder at yourself and the richness of life, which is come to you by the grace of God.
E. Carver McGriff.

Action Points and Discussion Questions

1. Compare yourself and your team with a Slinky.

2. Listen to "Bouncing Back," my podcast interview with David Beavers. Find it at HansFinzel.com/19

3. Sort out your absolute team principles from your relative programs.

4. Listen to my "Do Leaders Need Thick Skin?" podcast. HansFinzel.com/61

Chapter 7
"S" Is for Servant Attitude

Everyone seems to be throwing around the phrase, "servant leader." I think many misunderstand it. Some people think they are servant leaders but are far from it. "Frankly placing servant in front of leader sounds very spiritual but seems to have not done much good," says Duane Elmer in *Cross Cultural Servanthood* (Page 156).

What is a Servant Leader?

"The servant-leader is *servant first* ... It begins with the natural feeling that one wants to serve, to serve *first*. Then conscious choice brings one to aspire to lead. That person is sharply different from one who is *leader first*, perhaps because of the need to assuage an unusual power drive or to acquire material possessions. The *leader-first* and the *servant-first* are two extreme types." - Robert Greenleaf, The Servant Leader (1970)

Servant Leadership: *When the leader cares more about the good of the team than his or her own enrichment.*

Two most important passages in the New Testament on servant leadership:

- John 13:1-17 –

"Now that I, your Lord and Teacher, have washed your feet, you also should wash one another's feet. I have set you an example that you should do as I have done for you."

- Philippians 2:1-4

"Do nothing out of selfish ambition or vain conceit. Rather, in humility value others above yourselves, not looking to your own interests but each of you to the interests of the others. Have the same mindset as Christ Jesus...

 The Kernel of Wisdom: The servant-leader is *servant first* caring more about the good of the team than his or her own enrichment.

Servant Leadership In Action

Exercise: Can you think of a recent concrete illustration of when you (or someone you watched) performed a true act of servant leadership? Describe it here:

_____

_____

_____

_____

_____

_____

_____ .

Servant Leaders Are Shepherds – I Peter 5:1-3

Servant Leadership—shepherd	Self-Serving Leadership—Hired hand
It's all about "we"	It's all about "me"
I serve others	Others serve me
I am happy if the team scores	I'm happy when I score
I carry everyone in my heart	I ride on the shoulders of everyone else
The needs of others come first	My needs come first
I am here for our cause	I'm here for my career
I am a shepherd	I am a hired hand
I want to help you fulfill your dreams	I am here to pursue my dreams
Team Empowerment	Personal Enrichment
We share the credit for wins	I take the credit for wins

"A leader is like a shepherd. He/she stays behind the flock, letting the most nimble go out ahead, where upon the others follow, not realizing that all along they are being directed from behind." – Nelson Mandela

A False View of Servant Leadership

What it is *not*:

- You serve _____

- You do all the _____ work

- You work 24/7 for the _____

- You are _____

- Others _____ of you

- You carry the _____ on your back

- You are a _____

- You let others _____

- You have no _____

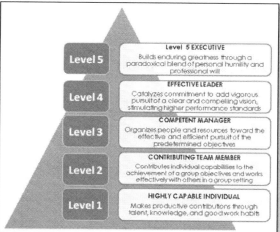

Action Points and Discussion Questions

1. How would you define servant leadership in your own words?

2. On a scale of one to ten, how well do you think you do in being a servant of your team?

3. Touching on the topic of *slave leadership*, list some of the unrealistic expectations that people have of you.

4. In light of your list under number three, how could you change your leadership style to add some boundaries yet continue serving your people?

Chapter 8
H" Is for Hands-Off Delegation

Sometimes there is a fine line between *empowering* your team and *frustrating* your team. If you try to control them too much, they feel controlled and frustrated. If you give them freedom to grow with the healthy delegation skills I unpack in this chapter, they really will grow as leaders and feel empowered.

Sloppy delegation is one of the greatest sins of leadership. There is no mistake a leader makes that seems to spread more misery to followers.

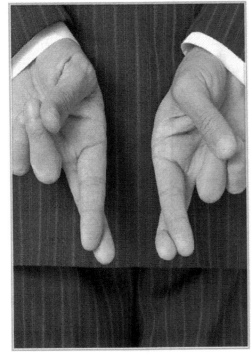

As I have studied delegation over the years, I have discovered four themes that occur with most leadership teams:

- _____ is one of the great cardinal sins of poor leadership.
- The lack of good delegation is rooted in_____ in the leader.
- Nothing frustrates those who work for you more than _____delegation with too many _____attached.
- Delegation should match each worker's _____- ability.

The Kernel of Wisdom: Great delegation is like great *discipleship*. We are actually developing the potential in others.

Why It's Hard To Delegate Well

1. Fear of _____

2. Fear of _____

3. Fear of _____

4. Unwillingness to _____

5. Fear of _____

6. Lack of _____

7. Fear of losing _____

8. Fear of _____

Four Questions That Every Follower Asks

1. What do you _____

2. Will you let me _____

3. Will you _____

4. Will you _____

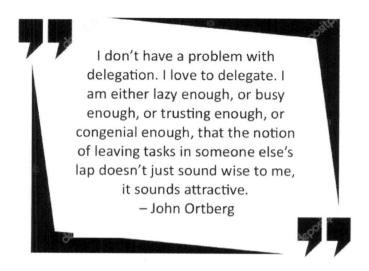

I don't have a problem with delegation. I love to delegate. I am either lazy enough, or busy enough, or trusting enough, or congenial enough, that the notion of leaving tasks in someone else's lap doesn't just sound wise to me, it sounds attractive.
– John Ortberg

Are you good at a lot of things?

It seems that more gifted and talented you are, the harder it is to be a great delegator. You can do a lot of things better than other people! That is one problem. Also, it seems that some insecure personality types(control freaks) really find it very hard to release work to others.
Great delegation is like great discipleship. We are actually developing the potential in others. Here are seven "wins" that occur when you learn to be a great delegator:

The Results of Great Delegation - Discipleship

- It _____people

- It _____ people

- It taps into the _____

- It builds a strong _____

- It spreads _____

- It empowers _____

- It's about _____ not _____

Action Points and Discussion Questions

1. Try a role-play experiment in delegation.

2. Listen to my two podcasts called "How to Be an Awesome Delegator—Part 1 and Part 2," HansFinzel.com/39 and HansFinzel.com/40

3. Review and discuss the list of the reasons why people don't delegate well.

Chapter 9
"I" Is for Integrity

The "I" in leadership stands for *integrity*. When we lose our integrity, we lose all credibility. People may still follow us because they have to, but it won't be a pretty picture. Integrity is about being complete and whole. It means that you are on the inside what you claim to be on the outside. You are not a poser who pretends to be something you are not. Integrity is also about honesty, ethics and being fair.

Sunk by Many Tiny Gashes

Scientists now say that a series of slits, not a giant gash, sank the Titanic. The opulent, 900-foot cruise ship sank in 1912 on its first voyage, from England to New York. Fifteen hundred people died in the worst maritime disaster of the time. The most widely-held theory was that the ship hit an iceberg, which opened a huge gash in the side of the liner. But an international team of divers and scientists recently used sound waves to probe the wreckage, buried in the mud under two and a half miles of water. Their discovery? The damage was surprisingly small. Instead of the huge gash, they found six relatively narrow slits across the six watertight holds. Small damage, invisible to most, can sink not only a great ship but a great reputation.

The Kernel of Wisdom: *"Above all else, guard your heart, For everything you do flows from it." Proverbs 4:23*

Finish Line Question

"How would you describe a successful life when you're looking back from the finish line?"

_____

_____

_____

_____

Words of wisdom from the marketplace and the ministry

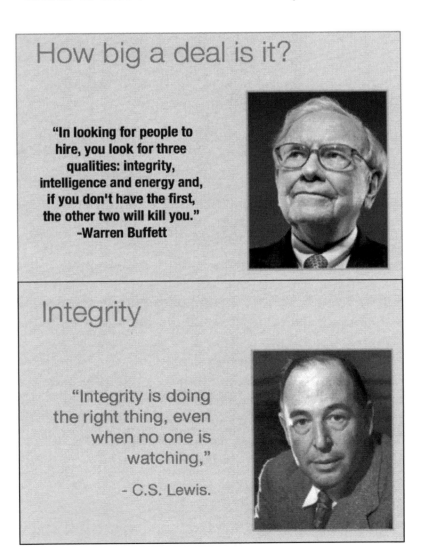

How big a deal is it?

"In looking for people to hire, you look for three qualities: integrity, intelligence and energy and, if you don't have the first, the other two will kill you."
-Warren Buffett

Integrity

"Integrity is doing the right thing, even when no one is watching,"

- C.S. Lewis.

Why Do People Follow You?

1. _____
2. _____
3. _____
4. _____
5. _____
6. _____

Six Barriers to Finishing Well

Dr. Bobby Clinton, who taught for many years at the Fuller School of Intercultural Studies, studied thousands of leaders over his lifetime. He studied scores of biblical leaders and many secular leaders as well as famous Christian leaders. *The Making of A Leader,* (NavPress revised 2012)

1. _____
2. _____
3. _____
4. _____
5. _____
6. _____

Action Points and Discussion Questions

1. Talk about the finish line question.
2. Areas of integrity that tempt you the most.
3. Regarding plateauing, check out my book, *The Power of Passion in Leadership.* Leadership *(Top Ten Enterprises Publishing, 2015).*
4. Read the story of Ananias and Sapphira in Acts 5:1-10.
5. Discuss how you can guard your hearts
6. What is more important, marking a mark or leaving a legacy?

Chapter 10
"P" Is for the Power of Humility

The "P" in the word L-E-A-D-E-R-S-H-I-P stands for the "Power of Humility." Pride has destroyed many a leader, but humility always wins the day.

Pride can creep in subtly. As the years have gone on and I have watched a lot of other leaders rise through the ranks, I have seen an interesting pattern. The more gifted they are, the more talented they are, the greater their education, the more tendency there is to rely on those skill sets to lead—leadership by a powerful personality and ego. Those will carry us for a while, but sooner or later, there comes a reckoning related to our arrogance. And if that reckoning does not come, neither will truly great leadership.

Learn a Lesson from Mighty Moses

I had to learn the same leadership lesson that Moses had to learn in Egypt after he tried to rescue his own people in his own strength. They rejected him outright: "Who made you ruler and judge over us? Are you thinking of killing me as you killed the Egyptian? Then Moses was afraid and thought, What I did must have become known" (Exodus 2:14 NIV).

He fled to the desert and, over the next forty years, God took the pride and arrogance completely out of him.

The Kernel of Wisdom: Of all the keys to great leadership, none is greater than *humility*.

What's So Great About Moses?

Of all the reasons I cite for great lessons we can learn from Moses, what are two that strike you the most helpful for your own work?

1. _____

2. _____

D. L. Moody said of Moses, "*Moses spent his first forty years thinking he was somebody. He spent his second forty years learning he was a nobody. He spent his third forty years discovering what God can do with a nobody.*" (D. L. Moody, quoted in Charles Swindoll, *Moses: A Man of Selfless Dedication*. Nashville: Thomas Nelson, 1999).

How would you describe a humble person? Three adjectives:

1. _____

2. _____

3. _____

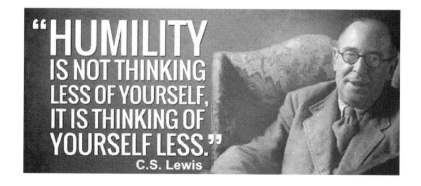

Truly A Better Way To Lead

To the elders among you, I appeal as a fellow elder and a witness of Christ's sufferings who also will share in the glory to be revealed: Be shepherds of God's flock that is under your care, watching over them—not because you must, but because you are willing, as God wants you to be; not pursuing dishonest gain, but eager to serve; not lording it over those entrusted to you, but being examples to the flock. And when the Chief Shepherd appears, you will receive the crown of glory that will never fade away.

In the same way, you who are younger, submit yourselves to your elders. All of you, clothe yourselves with humility toward one another, because,

"God opposes the proud but shows favor to the humble." I Peter 5: 1-5 NIV

Coming Full Circle Back to the Beginning

I started this book by looking at the letter "L" in leadership. Do you recall what it stands for? It stands for *listen* and *learn*, the two most important words in the leader's vocabulary. The first and most important mistake that new leaders need to avoid is lack of listening and learning. And do you see how pride gets in the way of both of these skills for the new leader? If you think you have all the answers, you won't listen. If you have not dealt with your pride, you certainly won't be learning new things. It is from a place of humility you can be a truly great lifelong leader that will make a great mark and leave a lasting legacy.

> A magnetic loyalty grows in followers who respond to humble leaders who lead with a passionate shepherd's heart. That is not to say that they cannot be men and women of great gifting and ability, but they don't overpower people with their talent. - Hans Finzel

Action Points and Discussion Questions

1. Do you have the blessing of being highly talented and gifted?
2. Watch the Steve Jobs commencement address. (Search YouTube)
3. Take a lesson from a domineering leader that you have worked under.
4. Like we talked about in chapter 9, do you care more to make a mark or leave a legacy?

Your Aha Moments

I have left this page intentionally blank so that you can write down some of the biggest "ah ha" moments from the presentation. What hit you the hardest? What did you find most useful? What are some of your most memorable takeaways?

Other Books by Hans Finzel

The Top Ten Mistakes Leaders Make
David C Cook   (Print, Kindle and audiobook)

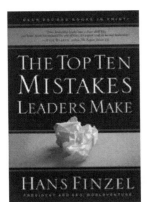

Although leadership is the hot topic on conference agendas and book tours, most people who find themselves in positions of leadership have little or no training for the role. They simply continue to make the same old mistakes.

With additional and newly updated material, this leadership classic reveals the most common errors that leaders consistently make-regardless of training or age-and the way to stop these bad habits from undermining their positive talents and accomplishments.

Whether you are leading a church, company, hospital, ministry, a Girl Scout troop, or your family, *The Top Ten Mistakes Leaders Make* is a must-read for anyone who wants to lead others effectively.

The Power of Passion in Leadership
Top Ten Enterprises (Print, Kindle and audiobook)

In this brand new book you will learn what it means to work in your "passion zone." Hans explains from his own career journey, how to find your passion zone and what action steps to take if you are far from that place of fulfillment. People love following leaders whose hearts are fueled by passion. This book will help you uncover what passion in your work really is, and how to find it, no matter what stage you are at in your career. The advice in this book is especially powerful for anyone in a role of leadership that is experiencing **boredom** or **burn out**. Life is too short to settle for less than the best—especially if we are called to lead other people.

Top Ten Leadership Commandments
David C Cook (Print and Kindle)

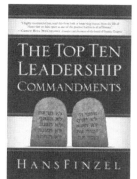

This leadership classic is based on the life and legacy of Moses. Hans says, "I happen to think he is one of the greatest leaders in history because he had such a tough leadership assignment but did not quit!"

The life of Moses provides a master study on what it means to be an effective leader. Consider his pedigree: Answered the call to do something beyond his means; stood his ground before kings; led millions of people on a journey across rivers and through deserts. Moses did this all with a dogged persistence that would not give up. You will discover a dynamic, effective tool for developing leadership skills, all built on the solid foundation of God's word.

Change is Like a Slinky
Moody Press Northfield (Print and Kindle)

This is a practical guide to navigate change in today's organizational climate. Change or perish: this is a current motto for leaders in all types of organizations.

But how does one adapt to such fast and furious change and effectively lead the organization through change?

Hans provides a proven strategy in Change is Like a Slinky, exploring the six major phases in the cycle of change. As he says, "Change is a lot like a Slinky... A slinky can be a lot of fun, but it is also completely unpredictable."

Instead of grudgingly wading through inevitable change, readers will find themselves equipped and fired up to tackle it head on.

Launch Your Encore
Baker Books (Print and Kindle)

No longer retiring at 65 and dying soon there after, people are ending up with a whole lot of life left after their main careers are over. A lot of boomers are asking the post career question, "What's next?" Most of us don't believe in the "R" word, traditional retirement. Launch Your Encore is the answer to the "what's next," question. We explore how to find adventure and purpose later in life with intentionality. There are dangers to avoid and adventures to explore. Our passion is to help you find meaning and purpose in your sixties, seventies, and eighties (What we have coined as the 60-80 window). With the average U.S. life expectancy reaching eighty, we are entering an exciting new life stage. It just might be that our final act is our greatest.

Unlocking The Scriptures
David C Cook (Print and Kindle)

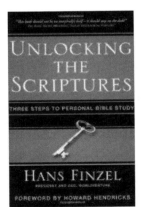

Even though there are many resources on Bible study methods, I fully recommend this book for the serious Bible student. This is a classic book on inductive Bible study.

This updated classic leads the reader through the inductive Bible study process, showing practically how to dig into serious Bible study on your own.

With this tool, Christians can learn to relevantly apply God's Word to their lives as His Spirit leads them personally, rather than as some other leader might direct. Unlocking the Scriptures provides practical examples that walk the reader through the steps of unpacking Scripture, using actual passages to practice. Free downloadable study guide and activities.

MillennialBOOM!
Top Ten Publishing (Print and Kindle)

What is the Millennial BOOM? It might just be the sound of warfare across the two largest generations in America today. Boomers number 76 million but Millennials are maxing out at 82 million! Is it possible to reduce the friction and respect each other?

Hans and Patrick Kelly wrote this book to break up the cold war in life and work with Boomers and Millennials everywhere.

What makes this book unique? It is co-written by a Boomer and a Millennial who actually respect each other and have learned to work well together!

- Learn about the five arenas of conflict that are the flashpoint between these two alienated generations.
- Understand the difference between the generations and identifying workable solutions.
- We all have stereotypes of each other's generation: Learn to lay aside condemnation and try a hand a collaboration!
- Proven strategies for getting along in the workplace—actually thriving together with respect for one another.
- Understand how best to assimilate Millennials into your workplace that is dominated by Boomers.

You can always find me at my website: HansFinzel.com

Made in the USA
Columbia, SC
10 October 2020